A Word From T...

First and foremost I would like to thank you for p... ...was never an easy decision to let people into the rollercoaster that is my life but I am glad you are here and I hope that you take away something from the words that form the verses that describe the most vivid parts of my life. There's no timeline order here, each verse just written as and when I decided to deal with each memory, each emotion. These poems were written from 2010 up to 2022 and are just a selection of many!

If you are able to relate to any of the words, I just want to send you love and hope. It will be ok. As the famous saying goes "if it's not ok, it's not the end" and I hope that you will find your ending and it will be one of happiness.

Can I say I have my happy ending?

No, not yet but I can say that life is so much happier than it has been and I have so much to be thankful for. I always try to focus on the here and now, on what I have rather than what I have lost. This has been helped by my personal spiritual journey (but that's another book entirely!)

After over forty decades of trauma my motto now is I will survive...

No Matter What, Come What May!

Sending much love to you all

Mantha xxx

"Revenge is surviving, getting out, and being a better person than you were, and breaking the cycle."

KRISTY GREEN

Be Careful What You Wish For!

It's a hard life, my life, eight years old
Still so young but a story to be told
You see she never really wants me now unless it's for her gain
She doesn't see how sad I am, how I feel the pain
She smacks me, she yells, she grabs me by the hair
She doesn't touch the other two, it just isn't fair
She tells me daily, she's going to send me away
Yes Please Mum, Please do it I pray
Thursday, Friday, Saturday, it's bingo night tonight
And then there'll be another man if the price is right
Lay in my bed listening to sounds a child shouldn't hear
Screams, Whips, Grunts, Groans, is there something to fear?
The baby wakes, I run to see, don't want her crying out
I don't want Mummy to get mad, I hate to hear her shout
Morning comes, its time for me to get them washed and fed
And make sure its quiet, Mum has a bad head
As I play at being Mummy, I dream of things afar
I want to be famous one day, I want to be a star
Slap, Reality, a blow to the head
Stop daydreaming child, do something useful instead
I love you mummy I really do but you make me cry
You make me wish such bad things,
you make me wish you'd die

I am a child, not a sink for your frustrations

- VINEET RAJ KAPOOR

Adult Versus Child

Adults hands slap, sting, pulling at my hair
Adults feet, kick, pushed into a chair
Adults mouth, screaming, I'm a nasty little cow
Adults ears, not hearing, how I'm sobbing now
Adults heart, so cold, why can't you just love me?
Adults mind, preoccupied, about a night out you see
Adults tongue, vicious, the words cut into me
Adults fists, below the ribs, no marks for them to see
Adults lies, to the school, when they ask is all okay
Adults threats, telling me, what to do and say...

Childs hands shaking, so scared inside
Childs feet, want to run, need to hide
Childs mouth, saying, Mummy I love you
Childs ears, not hearing, yes I love you too
Childs heart, broken, scarred, ruined altogether
Childs mind, memories that can't be erased not ever
Childs tongue, bitten, don't say a word
Childs fists, clenched, but the anger unheard
Childs frustration, fear of the hate
Childs lies, to her friends, yes my life is great
Childs threats? There's none, I am only eight...

Behavior is the language of trauma. Children will show you before they tell you that they are in distress.

Micere Keels

Uncle

Come here now, I have someone for you to meet
This, Children, is your Uncle Pete
He is chunky, sweaty, about six feet tall
His breath smells of pepper, just like that Uncle Paul
Or was it Uncle Reg? Or maybe Uncle Nick?
There's been so many of them, it makes me feel sick
The one who used to force me to climb up on his knee
And then he would stroke my hair with such a look of glee
The one who liked to hurt my Mum, to make her eyes go black
She really seemed to like that one, she always took him back
I would have liked a Daddy if the right one came along
But Mum never liked nice men, only the ones who did her wrong

*Child abuse casts a shadow
the length of a lifetime.*

Herbert Ward

I Miss You

Gone to soon, life just isn't fair
I can still picture you, stood over there
I'm sorry I didn't show just how I felt
I never got the chance to say you made my heart melt
Life became too much to bear, you couldn't take it anymore
Why the hell didn't you come to me? Ain't that what friends are for?
I never stopped loving you, not then, not ever
Haunting thoughts, you'd still be there, if we'd stayed together
My first true love, my Mr Right, the father of my son
We blew it, let it fall apart, the cold hard grief won
So now you're up there in another world, nothing to hurt you again, never
And yes time heals, life goes on, but I'll love you forever and ever

TO ANYONE OUT THERE WHO'S HURTING - IT'S NOT A SIGN OF WEAKNESS TO ASK FOR HELP. IT'S A SIGN OF STRENGTH.

- BARACK OBAMA

Turn It Around

You're evil, I hate you, you make my skin creep
You make me weak, vulnerable, you made my eyes weep
You took my dignity, my pride, my trust of all men
You hurt me, you scarred me, you made me cry again
You made me dirty, filthy, you took my self respect
You made me wretch, gag, you have that effect

You made me...STOP!!!

You made me turn it around
I made it about me, the strength that I found
I am strong, resilient, I won't weep, not now
I am proud, I am loved, and I trust somehow
I am pure, cleansed, my scars they fade
I am free, I can block out, the memories have decayed
I hope your conscience gives you hell each day
But me? Don't you worry, cos I am here to stay

*I was like,
"No, please stop"
He was like,
"No, you'll like it."*

Female student, Queens University of Charlotte

Feelings

A crowded room but here I am in need of a friend
One who really understands, one who doesn't pretend
Can you see this emptiness that's here deep inside?
The pain is raw, its real, its something I cannot hide
You empathise, you sympathise, you say you're always there
But you ask no questions, Can you not handle my emotions bare?
You don't know what to do or say or how to react
You ask how I am doing but do you want fiction or do you want fact?
I know its hard to deal with, the pain you see in me
But take solace because I know that one day I will be set free

"YOU DON'T DROWN BY FALLING INTO WATER.
YOU ONLY DROWN IF YOU STAY THERE."

-ZIG ZIGLAR

Grandad

From the day I was born, you were always there
Creating memories that we both could share
You loved to laugh, loved being with us all
If we needed you, we just had to call
You showed so much pride for the family you had
And we loved you too, so much Grandad
I hate the fact you had to go
Why so soon, I'll never know?
So now we're left with this empty space
Nothing or No-one can ever replace
I try to remember you will always be here
In my heart, In my dreams, behind every tear
I miss you so much, nothing feels right
I know you tried to stay, you put up a fight
We had so much left, we needed to do
There was so much more I needed to share with you
But I know with time, I can still do those things
Knowing you're right beside me no matter what life brings

When I think of all my blessings
You are one of them
Far from perfect but you saved me from so much
I love you Grandad

My Friend

What is the meaning of friendship?
How do you know that its true?
I don't believe I understood till the day I met you
You've helped me through the bad times, you've made the good times great
You've proved a million times to be a special mate
I'll never be able to show you just how much I care
I need you to know how much it means, knowing you're always there
I know our friendship will last forever, no matter what life throws
I look on you as my best friend, the family that I chose

Friendship is not one big thing- it's a million little things.

- PAULO COELHO

The Day

Do you ever sit and wonder where my life's at now?
Do you ever sit and wish you had never broken that vow?
Lying here its hard to forget the times we had as two
Scared I will never love again, the way I did with you
I sometimes imagine I hear you calling out my name
Then reality kicks in, telling me life will never be the same
You broke my heart, crushed me, left me so empty inside
Here I am, putting on an act and trying to protect my pride
People tell me that you are bad, that I'm better off without
But they don't know you like I did, how I felt when you were about
The truth is there though for me to see, you took me for a fool
Lied to me, abused my love and broke every goddamn rule
I will never forget the times we shared, the bonds that we once had
The day will come though, that I am sure, when it won't hurt like mad
Cos I am strong, I'll get over you, time will help me heal
And one day I know you will sit back and regret will be all that you feel
When that time comes, don't call on me cos there'll be no reply
Even though that I know deep down, I'll love you till I die

"Sometimes good things fall apart so better things can fall together."

Marilyn Monroe

Ethan Anthony

Ethan Anthony, my beautiful son
Your life cruelly snatched before it had begun
You fought for so long, went through it all
But heaven needed an angel, you received your call
Lying in my arms, so at peace and at rest
You'll never know how much it meant holding you to my chest
I told you that I loved you, that I needed you with me
Wishing for you to open your eyes and prove it was meant to be
You were so tiny yet perfect, ten fingers ten toes
Your tiny little furrowed brow, your Mummy's eyes and nose
You will always be my baby boy, created out of love
And I hope you can see how loved you are when you look down from up above
You're in my heart and in my thoughts no matter what I do
And I live for the day when I get reunited with you
Because when we meet again, I need to hold you tight
Need to hear you call me Mummy and give me kisses goodnight
But until then my little Angel, I know where you are
Looking over us, loving us all, the brightest ever star

*I carried you every second of your life,
and I will love you for every
second of mine.*

Unknown

One Day

Lying here empty, my thoughts full of you
Was there more I could have done? Something I didn't do?
Everytime they told me that you would lose the fight
You proved them wrong, gave a kick to show you were alright
All the bad times, you were there, with me all the way
Giving me courage, giving me strength, making me want to stay
Is that why you were sent? To help me with my fight?
If that's the case, why couldn't you stay, when everything went right?
You were my little hero, for months it was just me and you
But you need to know just how much others love you too
There's an empty space in our hearts, a hole that can never be healed
Our love for you will remain strong, the bond is truly sealed
I miss you Baby, the pain is so bad, I've cried so many tears
I just hope the hurt inside gets easier as we go through the years
Promise me that you're always close, never far away
Look over us all, the ones you love, till we meet again one day

*An angel, at the Book of Life,
Wrote down my baby's birth.
Then whispered as he closed the book,
"Too beautiful for Earth."*

Unknown

Our Boys

It's finally sinking in that you're really there
Not just a single baby but a beautiful pair
Words cannot express how much you already mean
So much love for two as small as a tiny bean
A symbol of the love that your Daddy and I share
The thought of losing you, more than I can bear
Names already picked, Logan and Chance
Created to complete, fulfil and enhance
Its going to be a fight of that there's no doubt
But I promise you this, you will be loved, adored, never go without
I try to imagine how you will be
A perfect mix of your Daddy and Me
The bond between the two of you must be so strong
Use that for each other, make sure nothing goes wrong
I love you my boys, more than I can say
Can't wait to meet you, all I can do is pray
I feel you growing inside me, it fills me with pride
But I know the fear and pain I feel is so hard to hide
So keep safe my babies, I'll see you soon
You are my everything, my sun stars and moon

How very quietly you tiptoed into our world, silently, only a moment you stayed. But what an imprint your footprints have left upon our hearts.

Unknown

Friday 13th

Friday 13th 2010, a day I never want to relive, never again
The day I lost my precious baby boys
Snatched from me, left with no choice
And now I sit three days on
Still not believing that you are both gone
This empty feeling deep inside
The hurt, the pain, I am trying to hide
I miss you so much, I miss the little things
The little wiggles, flutterings, the joy that it brings
You were so loved, craved by us all
But it wasn't meant to be, you both received your call
So we are left to cope with the gap left in our hearts
And the deep dark pain like being stabbed with darts
Whats left for us to do? What more can we say?
Except sleep tight, we love you, see you both one special day

Don't forget that when people lose a baby they aren't just losing a newborn. They are also losing their toddler taking their first step. Their infant starting to read. Their teenager graduating high school. Their grown child getting married to the love of their life..They are losing every magical moment... In the blink of an eye, the future was erased.

Zoe Clark-Coates

A Sign

Driving back home tonight along the motorway
We saw it there clear to see, the strongest brightest ray
Your Daddy turned to me and said "You see that's where they are"
I felt such a comfort to feel you near to me, not far
The brightest shining down from the skies, lighting up the way
A sign from you to say to us, we'll meet again one day
The hurt I feel the pain inside, I'm struggling to cope
But the sight I saw, soothed a little, gave me some hope
I miss you both so very much, I hope you feel it still
And I hope you feel all my love, the longing only you can fill
I miss you Chance and Logan, you're always in my heart
And there you will remain, until we are no longer apart

*Those we love never truly leave us.
There are things that death
cannot touch.*

Jack Thorne

Why I Love You So...

You asked me to explain just why I love you so
My reply to you at the time was "I really do not know"
I couldn't put into words how you make me feel
All I knew was that what I felt was the real deal
But then as I sat and thought about why and how
I realised just why it is, so let me tell you now
You make me smile everyday, make me warm inside
I have never felt so loved before, it shows in every kiss
Every moment we are apart, something feels amiss
I love the times we think alike, the same words come on out
I love the way you understand, what I am all about
You seem to know how I feel without me needing to say
And if I feel down and low, you take it all away
The special times we have had together really are the best
The bad times, made us strong, put us to the test
Your honesty means the world to me, I trust you with my life
I want to be your everything, I want to be your wife
Your funny ways, your gorgeous eyes, your smile that melts my heart
All of these little things, without them I'd fall apart
You see you really are the bestest friend that I have ever had
I even love those things you do that I claim drive me mad!
So there you have it, I've said it all, every word is true
The reason that I love you so, is just because you're you!

In all the world, there is no heart for me like yours. In all the world, there is no love for you like mine.

Maya Angelou

Insomnia

The darkness is around me, the silence is so loud
It works its magic through the night, it acts so bold and proud
Mind racing, pain chasing, energies collide
Here I am, Insomnia, from me you cannot hide
This way, that way, everything I try
Tiredness brings me down so low, I sob, I cry
One drug, two drug, three drug, four
The amount I take should have me falling to the floor
At last it comes, wraps itself around
I drift to the place where dreams are found
But then it happens, it all goes wrong
I get a rude awakening by the bird's morning song
I wait all day, watching the hours
As the effect of the night totally devours
Then at last, the time has arrived
To battle to sleep, but to be deprived
Why can't you please give me a break?
I just need some rest, for goodness sake
Just one whole night, filled full of dreams
I ask for too much, or so it seems

The scary thing about having insomnia
is not the hours lost for sleeping but the
re-run of thoughts you've been
trying to forget.

Unknown

Time

Nine, Ten, need my bed.
Tiredness pulsating through my head
Eleven, Twelve, toss and turn.
All my joints burn burn burn
One, Two, I manage to rest.
Then comes the pain inside my chest
Three, Four, watching the blackness around.
Lying listening to every sound
Five, Six, sleep starts to win.
But still I rouse at the drop of a pin
Time comes for the day to start,
I have nothing to give I am falling apart

INSOMNIA IS JUST ANOTHER WORD FOR CHIT CHAT WITH THE DEMONS DURING BEDTIME.

DANIEL SAINT

Welcome, Come In

Welcome, Come in, take a step into my life
Come and see it, feel it all, my trouble and my strife
How each waking day is one filled with pain
How my life feels to me, as miserable as the rain
The tiredness, encases me, swallows me up whole
Every movement, every step, everything takes its toll
The butterfly rash all over my face
You say its not bad but I know that's not the case
I ache, I hurt, my joints scream out loud
I need help, I need help but I feel too proud
I want to live, I want to die, I don't know how I feel
This existence that I have, its not life its an ordeal

Dear Lupus,
Because of you, I live in pain when I shouldn't have to. Because of you I will never know what life without medication is. I wouldn't wish you upon anyone, but I want to thank you. I thank you because you showed me I could. You showed me I was stronger than I knew. You proved to me I was a fighter and a survivor. You showed me that I still could. So, I may not like you, but I want to thank you. Sincerely, One of your millions of victims who will be ok!

Unknown

Today, Tomorrow

Today I feel strong, today you won't make me cry
Today I won't keep asking, over and over, why?
Today I have the energy to do just as I choose
Today its like I have extended that, normally so short, fuse
Today I am in control, you cannot dictate to me
Tomorrow? Well that's a different story,
we'll just have to wait and see

No matter how broken you feel today, tomorrow will be a better day.

Unknown

Misery

Its dark, cold and lonely here
Thoughts corrupt, engulfed in fear
The grip so tight, no way out
Suffocation, deprivation, full of self-doubt
Whispers, voices, all around
Hush they are coming, make not a sound
Cover your ears, close your eyes
There's no end, its lies lies lies
Misery, gloom, a bitter end
There's no way to escape for you, my friend

Misery loves company don't let it find you

-Queenk Chelsea

You Don't See

"Hey Manth, you look well"
You haven't noticed how my feet swell
You don't see the way I wince in pain
You never heard me say how tired I am again

"Manth you look great without all your hair"
What if it was you, would you not care?
Would you not want to curl up and hide?
Keep well away from the world outside?

"What you need love, is lots of rest"
How can you tell me that you know what's best?
What I need is to be understood and heard
Not to be stared at for being absurd

"Mantha I don't know how you carry on"
But you say I look healthy, like nothings wrong
You don't see this horror in me
The beast that attacks, it won't leave me be

"Tell me Mantha, what can I do?"
All that I ask is that I can turn to you
That I feel that you are always there
To hold me up through each Lupus flare

I don't mean to offend or throw back your kind ways
But your advice isn't always wanted on those bad days
To understand Lupus you have to live through the shit
But I wouldn't wish it on anyone so let me teach you bit by bit

Sometimes you will be in control of your illness and other times you'll sink into despair, and that's OK! Freak out, forgive yourself, and try again tomorrow.

- Kelly Hemingway

Beast

A new day starts but yesterday is still here
I haven't slept a wink due to pain, or was it fear?
The alarm starts to screech, ringing in my ears
As I move the pain comes and so do the tears
Tentative steps towards the day ahead
Planning every moment before I've even left my bed
Wouldn't it be easier to just stay here for the day?
And let the beast do what it wants, let it eat away
The sun shines through the blind, filling me with dread
For whilst others get a tan, I get a horrid rash instead
I've worked it all out now, I need to pace myself till noon
I may be able to meet my friend as long as I save a spoon
But before I even get to lunch I need to prep myself
I take the handful of those horrible meds that help me with my health
I dream of an existence being Lupus free
Where I could have a life that revolves only around me
But it seems that this indeed is my destined path
Living with the wolf inside and it's evil wrath

*To understand the relevance of the spoon, please research The Spoon Theory

"I HAD TO REALLY LEARN
HOW TO LOOK AT MYSELF
IN THE MIRROR ON THE
DAYS WHERE I FELT THE
UGLIEST AND STILL
BELIEVE THAT I WAS WORTHY"

UNKNOWN

Fight

Sometimes I sit wondering, why has this happened to me?
Why not pick on somebody else, why not leave me be?
The pain is unbearable, in my body, in my mind
Worrying constantly, what else will they find?
I lie awake most nights, wondering will I die?
How will I cope with having to say goodbye?
I'm trying to face the biggest fight of my life
Sometimes it feels like I'm being stabbed with a knife
I will beat this disease, this badness inside
Even though I know it'll be a long bumpy ride
I have too much to live for, my family and friends
This is one fight that never ever ends

"Chronic illness will test the vow in sickness and in health and can either make or break a relationship."

Danielle Myers

My Angels

Why does it hurt so deep inside?
Never ending amounts of tears I've cried
The pain as raw as the day you went
Not fading at all, I feel totally spent
Birthdays, Christmas… it hits so hard
I can't send you a gift, write you a card
I can't hear you call "Mummy" and ask for my love
I just have to hope you feel it from up above
Nothing and Nobody can ever fill your space
I wrap your memories in a warm embrace
You are in my day, morning through night
The brightest stars, my shining light
I love you so much and I long for the day
When I can hold you in my arms, forever to stay

*"There is no heartbeat."
4 words. 4 words to end the
life I had. 4 words to change who I was.
It will never be the same again.
I will never be the same again.*

Kerin Lee

Misunderstood

All I did for you, I did because I cared
Purely because of the friendship, that we had shared
I am always thankful for all you did for me
But it hurts to feel, I have been forgotten so easily
One day you will see that you got it all so wrong
That I didn't deserve to be shut out, no hurt deserved all along
You misunderstood what I tried to say
Willing to throw our friendship away
Maybe I never really meant that much
But when there's truth in what's said, the nerve hurts to touch
Too proud to admit that beneath it all, you feel guilt
Too stubborn to make a move, let bridges be rebuilt
Empty promises made and broken, it cuts through my heart
Misunderstood, wrongly taken, a friendship blown apart

*Friendship means understanding, not agreement.
It means forgiveness, not forgetting.
It means the memories last, even if contact is lost.*

Unknown

Turned Tables

It's funny how it changes when the tables turn
You cannot predict how it will be, you have to live and learn
In an ideal world, it would be simple and true
That people would return the love and care shown by you
All the times I listened, when you had so much to say
I didn't get offended all those times you pushed me away
I gave advice when needed, an ear for you to bend
I tried my best to be for you, a true and loyal friend
Things have changed a little bit, now it's me feeling hurt and pain
It's me unable to see the sunshine through all the rain
But things seem to be different, it's different rules for me
I am not allowed to feel the upset, pain and the misery
I didn't mean to be so sharp or come across as blunt
But I didn't think that with a friend like you, I needed to put on a front
I don't need sympathy, I don't want your pity
Just your understanding when I'm feeling kind of shitty
But now the tables have turned, it's quite obvious to see
That what was expected by you, doesn't apply to me
You can't just be there when everything's good and okay
True friendship should be there for every kind of day

You don't lose friends, because real friends
can never be lost.
You lose people masquerading as friends,
and you're better for it

Unknown

Happy Birthday

At the crem today I wasn't sure what to do
I bet people thought I was crazy, sat there talking to you
Remembering the good times, thinking back to the bad
Of all the tears of laughter, of the tears when we were sad
I can picture you now, those piercing eyes
Of all the times we went through, those goddamn goodbyes
But it was different one day, it was the final farewell
Nobody expected it at all, you hid it so well
The anger was there but now it's all gone
But the tears, they still come each time I hear our song
There is a special place in my heart, just for you
And you are with me in every little thing I do
Happy Birthday G, wherever you may be
You will always be loved, remembered and cherished by me

If you are feeling overwhelmed about anything in life please talk to someone.
If you feel unable to talk to family or friends then please call the Samaritans
Free Call - 116 123. (UK)

*It isn't that you didn't reach for them.
It's just that it was too hard to see your hand
in the blackness.*

Unknown

I Wish...

I wish you could tell me exactly how you feel
I wish I knew if you understand what's real
I wish your kisses were given freely
I wish I could hug you, oh so closely
I wish I could see the world through your eyes
I wish I could stop your screams and your cries
I wish I knew why you get so upset
I wish for once, we could just forget
I wish Autism didn't rule our life
I wish your pain didn't cut like a knife
I wish to tell you how very special you are
I wish for a cure, every night, on a star

*Autism, like a rainbow, has a bright side and
a dark side
and even though it can mean rough weather,
it can be beautiful!*

Stuart Duncan

Young Love

I really was a fool to run away from a guy like you
But I didn't know who I was or what was best to do
My heart was empty, grieving, the pain it felt so raw
I was crying out for your love, I needed so much more
We had something special, my first true love
But fate came and ruined it, that force from above
Our baby had been taken, our dreams ripped in two
We should have been together, I was there, where were you?
I needed you to hold me, tell me everything's okay
To wipe my tears, kiss my head, take the pain away
But you let me down, you flew miles away to stay
Left me crying all night long, struggling to get through the day
So I left, went away from you, without a word to say
I am sorry that I hurt you I know I broke your heart
And I want you to know I never forget, even after all the years apart
We were young and foolish, we ruined something great
If only older and wiser, we would have learned to communicate
But looking back it's clear that things turned out for the best
It proved we weren't strong enough to withstand the test
I am so glad you found happiness, you're worth your weight in gold
Thank you for being a part of my life and the precious memories I hold

A first love always occupies a special place.

Lee Konitz

Jane

When I look at my family now, I know it's thanks to you
You taught me what a family was, you showed me what to do
Fun, Laughter, Memories more than a many
Being there to love and care, giving your last penny
Making time for each other, no matter what
Nobody left out, nobody forgot
Christmas memories follow me now, us all cramped together
Happy pictures in my mind, engrained there forever
You treated me like your own, showed so much love and care
Taught me what a family was, made me more aware
Watching I always knew I wanted to be like you
To have a family and to treasure them, a deep love so true
I feel so lucky to have had you, come into my life
When I left leaving you all cut me like a knife
I want to say Thank You from the bottom of my heart
For the love, care and guidance you gave from the start
At 16 you gave me a real family of my own
Made me realise I could love, I didn't have to be alone
You showed me how a mother should be, giving love not pain
And I promised that I would never be in that life again
I swore my future children would have all they need and more
Because of you Jane... and all that you stood for
You are a true angel, all of you are
I think of you often, love and miss you from afar

*We all need someone who inspires
us to do better than we know how*

- anonymous

Just Another Shift...

The doors swing open, the trolley flies in
My heart starts to race, where do we begin?
Is he breathing? Is he bleeding? What can I do?
I can see his family watching, praying he'll pull through

The monitors are on now, drips all start to run
This guy's had a battle, I guess the other man won
Slowly his vitals begin to look okay
It looks like he's going to live to see another day

Next comes a child, just three years old
Her Mummy thought it was nothing but a cold
I lift her vest, the signs are all there
This baby's struggling to breathe in the air

The doctors tube her while I find a vein
Time is against us, I hate causing her pain
The machines take over, letting her rest
This girls put our skills fully to the test

Pushing her cot up to intensive care
You can't help but feel that life is unfair
Comforting her Mummy, knowing I'm unheard
I can't promise it'll be okay, I can't give my word

All through my shift I wonder how they are
Adrenalin still pumping as I leave towards my car
Then by the doors I hear the Mum call my name
"She's going to be ok, the miracle it came"

What a feeling of pure relief
Knowing it could so easily have been grief
The guy is okay too, he just needs some care
But what a feeling it is, knowing it's because I was there

There doing a job like no other
Saving a son, a dad, a brother
You can't save them all, this is true
But there's so many still here because of what we do

The best way to find yourself is to lose yourself in the service of others.

Mahatma Gandhi

Romance

Is it too much to ask, for a little romance?
For a dreamy walk, for a slow dance
Chocolates, cards or maybe a rose
That impromptu kiss on the top of my nose
That date you planned all alone
That soppy text sent from your phone
That letter you wrote, long or short
It doesn't matter, at least you thought
That bath you ran without me knowing
Candles and music as the water is flowing
Days out, nights in, filled with laughter
Is there really such a thing as happy ever after?
A meal for two as a nice surprise
That rush of love as I gaze into your eyes
Strolling along a beach, hand in hand
Laying in your arms on the golden sand
Sunrises, sunset, watching them together
With the one that your heart will belong to forever
I don't believe in fairytales or knights who save the day
I just wish for that special love to me shown to be in some way

'To love and be loved is to feel the sun from both sides.'

DAVID VISCOTT

Karma

I have needed surgeries, all because of you
Because of your need to abuse and all you put me through
You got your kicks, it made you feel at ease
Shame that to get your thrill you had to scar my knees

When I told you no, you didn't like that much
How dare a girl like me not want your touch
So you decided to make it count, make it one to remember
Ruined me, tore me apart, made me hate November

Life changing injuries is the technical term for what you've done to me
You see now I have to use a tube just to help me pee
The unspeakable things you did to me, the tools you chose to use
I remember everything, every pain, every cut, every bruise

For so long you had a hold even though I was free
Scared whilst I was hiding, would you find me?
In time with help, I remembered who I was before
Each day I learned to start to trust a little more
Look at me now I am surrounded by love, I am happy at last
And you? You're where you belong, stuck in the past

Don't get me wrong there's always the odd trigger
A smell, a noise, a little anxiety that suddenly gets bigger
But I find my man, my safe place
The one who showed me that I am not a disgrace
He doesn't see me as dirty, as damaged goods all wrecked
He showed me that love is about affection and respect

I hear that karma has taken her time, but she's made up for it to be fair
Given you your own life changing experiences to bear
Don't you dare look at yourself with pity, for yours was just back luck
You changed my life, changed my body forever and You didn't give a……

"Karma has no menu; you get served what you deserve"

Unknown

He Sees Me....

He sees me

He sees me, the real me.. the one I try to hide

He sees me, really sees when I disguise my pain due to pride

He sees me, truly, despite my body attacking itself

He sees me, completely, he's not put off by my health

He sees me, wholly, not the parts trauma left broken

He sees me, he sees all the things I leave unspoken

He sees me, as I am, imperfect scarred and in defeat

He sees me and he loves what he sees and makes me feel complete

He sees me.

"The greatest happiness of life is the conviction that we are loved;
loved for ourselves, or rather, loved in spite of ourselves."

VICTOR HUGO

My Pride, My Joy

My pride, my joy, that's what you are

My biggest achievements ever by far

I love you all so much, you make me proud each day

Becoming strong clever women, beautiful in every way

Together, we have come through the good and the bad

You always pick me up whenever I feel sad

I love each of you with every bit of my heart

You are always with me, even if we're apart

My Daughters, so precious, my everything

Thank-you for the love and happiness you bring

Words are not enough to express the unconditional love that exists between a mother and a daughter.

-Caitlin Houston

Lost, Found...Lost Again

Growing up I always felt that void
But when I asked questions people got annoyed
Were you not bothered when I came along?
Was it me? Did I do something wrong?

I found you once when I was just fourteen
Knocked on your door, you really wasn't keen
So again, rejected, I walked away
The pain hidden, nothing to say

In time I found you again, reached out with hope
Please don't reject me I just won't cope
This time you allowed me into your life
I felt accepted by you and by your wife

For a couple of years all was good
At last I had a dad, like all kids should
Rejection forgotten, I loved you so much
Then you backed away, stopped keeping in touch

Third times a charm or so they say
Third time of me being heartbroken this way
Never again, will you hurt my heart
I don't need a dad, we are better off apart

But it's not that easy, the thoughts still race
Wanting answers to questions I can't face
Why Dad? Why didn't you care about me
What about my girls and their hurt you didn't see

Then the message comes, telling me you're sick
If I want to see you I'd have to travel quick
But how could I do that, rush to you once more
When the wounds are so fresh, weeping and raw

You had told them all you wanted to die
It seemed that fate was happy to comply
Now it's too late, you're not here, you've left
Mixed emotions run through me, I feel bereft

Now I'll never have the answers that I crave
Why you didn't return all the love and loyalty I gave
Father by name but you were never a dad
I tried so many times, gave you all that I had

I hope you learnt lessons and see where you failed
How you lost me as a daughter, how that ship sailed
And in your next life I hope you do it right
Show your children love, make sure you put up a fight

How do I feel now, now you're not here
Confused, empty, still shedding a tear
The feeling of being rejected once, is enough to cause distress
But three times over, three times I went through that mess

Lost, found.. then lost again
I must have been insane
Should have seen from the start, it wasn't meant to be
You never wanted it "Dad", you never wanted me

There is nothing worse than a man that can be everything to everybody else except a father to their own child.

Unknown

Five Days Out Of Seven

I always felt like you saved me, pulled me out of hell
And for five days out of seven, I was happy, I felt so loved as well
But then the patterns started, that I hadn't seen before
When on your days off together, you would drink till you fell to the floor

Sometimes you were just silly, made me laugh out loud
You would get all soppy tell me how you were proud
But then there was the flip side, the side that hurt me bad
The times you made me see, things to make a child so sad

Bickering together, winding up the gears
Until the explosion, the pinnacle point nears
Screams, shouts, words so full of hate
Punches, kicks, headbutts… so angry and irate

Blood, smears of it… smashed glass everywhere
Whilst I watch hidden, between the bannisters on the stair
My heart pounding, tears streaming, not knowing what to do
That time I called the police, she lied and covered for you

Learning to fear the middle of the week
Two days off work, to relax so to speak
But those two days became whisky filled feuds
I hated the eggshells of the ever- changing moods

For those two days I wanted to run way
But then peace would be restored, come Friday
Teachers, Social Workers all came and asked
I never let on, I kept it all masked

Growing up I told myself that I would never live this life
Never would my husband lift a hand to his wife
Why didn't she leave? How could she stay?
Little did I know that I'd find out firsthand one day

"AS AN ALCOHOLIC YOU WILL VIOLATE YOUR STANDARDS QUICKER
THAN YOU CAN LOWER THEM."

- ROBIN WILLIAMS, WEAPONS OF SELF-DESTRUCTION.

History Repeated

I said I would never allow this, that I would never stay
After years of watching DV, like hell would I live that way
Be a punchbag like I'd seen whilst I was small?
But it's different for me, it's not the same at all

You see the thing is, he doesn't mean it, he told me that for sure
And he told me he loved me as I cleaned my blood off the door
I just press his buttons, I make him so mad
Then after, it's so awful for him, it makes him feel sad

It's only because he cares so much, that's what makes him switch
Or other times it's just because I'm such a stupid bitch
I deserve it all, anyone would say so, he said
As he punches me so hard, my body flies across the bed

Sometimes I think back to times when I was small
To what I used to promise myself when I thought about it all
Never would I allow, history to be repeated
Never would I end up, curled in a ball, defeated

Then one day something made me find my will
When I found out he's hit my girl, I feel like I want to kill
Within days of finding out, I made my plans so quick
With me, the girls and black bags, I drove far away, feeling sick

Then and only then, I realised my own strengths
Holding so much guilt, that it took him going to such lengths
It took him hurting my baby, to escape from all that pain
But I made my vow, history will never be repeated again

Domestic violence causes far more pain than the visible marks of bruises and scars. It is devastating to be abused by someone that you love and think loves you in return.

Unknown

Trauma Bingo

So much has happened in my 44 years
Intense pain, grief and hurting, so many tears
Many say it's crazy, for one person to have to bear
So much less than others, how can that be fair?

I try to make light of it, play it down a bit
But reality is my friend, my life has seen some shit
If we were to play trauma bingo, most would mark off just a few
I reckon I'd be close to a full house with all that I've been through

Let's go for the line with neglect, abuse, distress
DV and alcoholism completes that absolute mess
For the full house we may as well go in hard
Add rape, baby loss and incurable illnesses to the bingo card

One full house completed but there's no great win here
Just scars, mental and physical, and an underlying fear
Why do I have so much to bear? I guess we will never know
But I really wish I didn't have the markers to play this trauma bingo

*A note to anyone who needs to hear it:
We don't "get over" or "move on" from our trauma.
We are forced to make space for it.
We carry it.
We learn to live with it.
And, sometimes we thrive in spite of it.*

Unknown

A Different Kind Of Spirit

Since being a young girl I was different to the rest
I had a special friend, to help get things off my chest
His name was Joseph, he was caring and kind
Nobody else could see him but I didn't mind

He would give me advice, help me on my way
I was never alone, he would always stay
An imaginary friend that's what they all said
Little did they know it was me talking to the dead

Life carried on, troubles came and went
Joseph remained, love and guidance he sent
He taught me lessons different from before
About life never ending, about me doing more

My journey progressed, I learned so much more
And the more I believed, the more I heard and saw
In time I found my calling, knew where I was meant to be
Using my skills to help reunite family

Over 300 people have gained comfort, its true
I've proven to them, that spirits are around you
Messages given, that I could never have known
Passing on love via the spiritual phone

More guides have joined my life, so grateful for their call
Helping me to prove that people don't die at all
Life is eternal, they never completely went
So many people now believe from proof that I've sent

Souls, spirits, they will live forever and a day
They like to come chat, they always have lots to say
On a different plane but able to be around
Showing a love, so deep, a love so profound

I saw the light, knew I needed to share
To share the knowledge, make others aware
They may have left physically, their body has gone
But the important part of every person will always live on

"You have to grow from the inside out.
None can teach you, none can make you spiritual.
There is no other teacher but your own soul."

- Swami trekananda

Detrimental Love

Life has been a struggle, all uphill most the way
But even through it all, love managed to stay
I still love and care, my heart still beats
Despite all the hurt, despite all the defeats

I always mull it over, I tend to overthink
How do I survive? Why didn't I sink?
I've seen so much bad, my hearts been torn in two
But I still manage to allow, love to shine on through

I'm a person who cares deeply, will always put you first
Will see the good in you, even if you're at your worst
I get hurt by people, more times than a few
Still I keep on loving, cos that's just what I do

Love and light defeats all bad, at least that's what they say
I live by this as much as I can, I try to think this way
But bad stuff keeps on hitting, from the left, the right and above
But you know, no matter what, I will still continue to love

*Love doesn't hurt you. A person that doesn't know how to love hurts you.
Don't get it twisted.*

Tony Gaskins

The Good, The Bad, The Ugly

Manic highs, desperate lows
Which one today, god only knows?
Will we be walking on eggshells, talking to a wall
Will you be hyper, so intense, no rational at all

Mental health matters, I couldn't agree more
I've watched PTSD and Bipolar knock you to the floor
Watching you slide, helpless to make it stop
Seeing you so tired of being manic, you literally drop

Trying to forgive when you've hurt me, all the tears I've cried
I know it's not you, it's the illness that's inside
Making decisions that you wouldn't normally make
Actions through an episode, making a huge mistake

It's like there's three men, in this life we live
The good I love, the bad and ugly I have to forgive
I have to tell myself that the real you is there
Hidden behind the actions of a man who doesn't care

Over the years we've gained ourselves hope
Watched for the signs, learned how to cope
Now you know when you are fighting the fight
And you try to get through it, to get yourself right

I'm so proud of you, for all you've overcome
You won't let it be an excuse, unlike some
There's no grudges now, no disgrace
Together we stand, together we face

"What goes up must come down."
Mania causes people with bipolar illness to climb higher and higher and then crash like a wave rolling into the shore.

- TROY STEVEN

One In Four

The statistics say one in four
So I thought, after me, that there would be no more
Surely it would never strike a family again
No need to make them relive the pain

No means No! I had begged and cried
He wouldn't stop no matter how much I tried
Made me feel dirty, so sick, so vile
It was my fault, I went into denial

Time passes, scars start to heal
I have move on, try to forget how I feel
It happened, it was hell, it tore me apart
It sits heavy, a weight in my heart

Then one day, as years have gone by
I get the news that makes me want someone to die
My girl, my baby… different male, same ordeal
This cannot be happening, this cannot be real

The statistics say one in four
That's not accurate, there's been a flaw
In this house the numbers don't fit
Two in four have been through this shit

Police, forensics, court rooms again
It's happening all over, I'm feeling her pain
Did I fail her? Was there something I didn't do
How can she go through all of this too

When it happened to me it hurt like hell
But nothing hit as hard as seeing her go through it as well
I give her my support, I'm there by her forever
Trauma pulled us closer together

"We must send a message across the world that there is no disgrace in being a survivor of sexual violence - the shame is on the aggressor."

Angelina Jolie

If It's Not Ok, It's Not The End

So much has happened in just one life
So much pain, loss, trouble and strife
But still the smile manages to appear
Even when it's behind a heartbroken tear

When I get knocked down, I get back up again
My family, my friends, they all keep me sane
Still I have so much I need to face
Fear, it's a feeling I've had to learn to embrace

Lessons learned from every ordeal
How to think, how to react, how to feel
I go to bed every night and pray
That I will open my eyes to a brand new day

Life is uncertain, there's no guarantees
Fate comes along and does as it please
But together we stand, united by love
We get through each hurdle, every strike from above

Surrounded by support, it's how I cope
Different people give me all kinds of hope
So thank you all family, friend
And remember, if it's not ok… it's not the end

EVERYTHING WILL BE OKAY IN THE END
IF IT'S NOT OKAY, IT'S NOT THE END.

- JOHN LENNON

The Final Word… For Now!

If you've made it to the end of this book, thank you!

I realise it's not all fluffy clouds and rainbows but if it was it wouldn't be a very accurate representation of my life.

It was hard to know how much to put into this book, there's so many more poems about so many more events but I wanted to just give an insight with this book as there are plans for a biography being spoken about so I wanted to leave some of the details for that.

Everything I have written about is real, it's been a part of my life. I've often said that if I wrote a book people would think it was fiction because how can that amount of trauma happen to just one person? It's just not possible, is it?

Unfortunately, yes it is… and it still goes on now. Life keeps throwing challenges my way but I will not be beaten!

I'm helped by my family, my friends and my spiritual journey (I touched on that a little but there's a whole story in that alone!)

You may ask why I released this book… well it all began when a counsellor suggested I write my emotions out, then when she saw the results she told me that I should do something with the poems.. that it could help others maybe.

So here it is, the first part to me opening up to you - My Life, My Verse - the start of more to come and I hope you will stay on the rollercoaster with me.

If you have survived any of the subjects I discuss in this book and would like to talk, my email is always open to you. You can contact me on MyLife_MyVerse@outlook.com

Your support in buying this book means the world to me

Thank you from the bottom of my heart

Love Mantha xxx

Printed in Great Britain
by Amazon